To:

From:

45. A man over 30 should never:

Determine cleanliness of clothing by the sniff test.

46. A man over 30 should never:

Antagonize zoo animals.

47. A man over 30 should never:

Drink Depth Charges or do Jello Shots.

48. A man over 30 should never:

Spend an entire conversation reciting lines from movie dialogue instead of actually discussing something.

49. A man over 30 should never:

Go on spring break to hit on 18-year-olds.

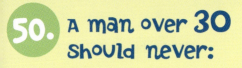

50. A man over 30 should never:

Play videogames until crippled by carpal tunnel.

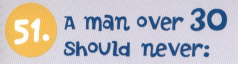

51. A man over 30 should never:

wear leather pants.

Grown-ups should never...

52. Follow Jimmy Buffett on tour.

53. Grown-ups should never:

use phrases like "fo' shizzle" and "da 'hood."

54. Grown-ups should never:

Go punk.

(we repeat: The '80s are over!)

55. Grown-ups should never:

Add the word "like" to, like, anything they say.

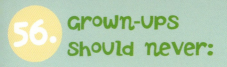

56. Grown-ups should never:

Dive into mosh pits or body surf at concerts.

57. Grown-ups should never:

Ask parents for $20 to go out for dinner.

58. Grown-ups should never:

Text, IM, or e-mail NE1 using 2 many net abbreviations. LOL CU ZZZ

59. Grown-ups should never:

Indulge in bubblegum—either the chewing or the listening kind.

60. Grown-ups should never:

Display theme park paraphernalia in their homes or on their bodies.

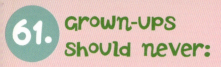

61. Grown-ups should never:

Attempt to audition for "American Idol."

62. Grown-ups should never:

Bite their nails and chew down their cuticles.

63. Grown-ups should never:

use "peace" as a greeting.

64. Grown-ups should never:

Buy an outfit for a night, wear it with the tags still on, then return it.

44. A man over **30** should never:

wear anything with velcro.

65 Things NOT to Do After Age 30

Claudine Gandolfi

Illustrated by Barbara McGregor

PETER PAUPER PRESS, INC.
White Plains, New York

Thanks to my sister Michele for her assistance in pointing out what the "old people" are trying to pull off.

Illustrations copyright © 2007 Barbara McGregor
Designed by Heather Zschock

Copyright © 2007
Peter Pauper Press, Inc.
202 Mamaroneck Avenue
White Plains, NY 10601
All rights reserved
ISBN 978-1-59359-863-1
Printed in China
14 13

Visit us at www.peterpauper.com

Introduction

You've laughed at some, cringed at many, perhaps dated one or two. But let's face it—you're likely to have committed "forever-young" faux pas yourself! (Yes, you!) And when bad bloopers happen to good people, they must be told!

This handy guide to the brave new world of adulthood will pry your fingertips from the windowsill of endless youth, and beat back the demons of

denial. Once you've hit the Big 3-0, no one will be fooled by bubblegum or cries of "Freebird!"

Relinquish the rubber bracelets. Kiss Hello Kitty goodbye. Deep six the Xbox. Abstain from that air guitar!

Maturity is calling. And it's asking for you by name.

A woman over 30 should never...

1. Dot her "i"s with circles or hearts.

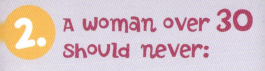

2. A woman over 30 should never:

wear glittery nail polish.

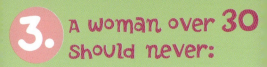

3. A woman over 30 should never:

wear anything with Hello Kitty on it.

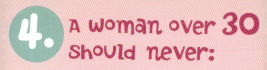

4. A woman over 30 should never:

wear a skirt that's shorter than the height of her shoe heel.

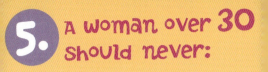

5. A woman over 30 should never:

Pierce anything other than her ears.

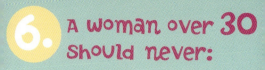

6. A woman over 30 should never:

See TITANIC more than once.

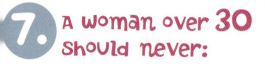

7. A woman over 30 should never:

Get a lower back tattoo.

8. A woman over 30 should never:

Blame anything on "baby fat."

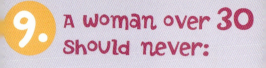

9. A woman over 30 should never:

Put her hair in pigtails.

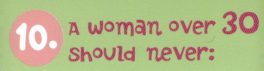

10. A woman over 30 should never:

Own a bike with a basket or tassels.

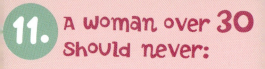

11. A woman over 30 should never:

Go to the bathroom in groups.

12. A woman over **30** should never:

Try to get back into her prom dress.

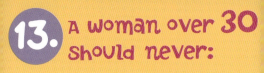

13. A woman over 30 should never:

make cupcakes for a party that doesn't revolve around kids.

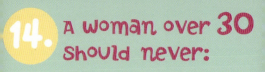

14. A woman over 30 should never:

Decorate with stuffed animals.

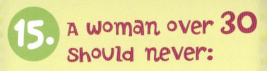

15. A woman over 30 should never:

Sport anything decorated with unicorns, flying horses, or rainbows.

16. A woman over 30 should never:

Go braless, no matter her cup size.

17. A woman over 30 should never:

wear flip-flops in the office.

18. A woman over 30 should never:

Play with her hair.

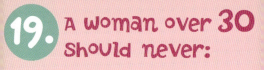

19. A woman over 30 should never:

wear butterfly clips or thumb rings.

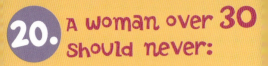

20. A woman over 30 should never:

Expect Daddy to get her car fixed, towed, or purchased.

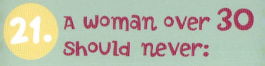

21. A woman over 30 should never:

Buy a "Happy Meal" for herself.

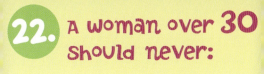

22. A woman over 30 should never:

wear a pair of pants that she has to lie down to zip.

23. A woman over 30 should never:

Believe what salespeople tell her about how she looks in that outfit.

24. A woman over 30 should never:

Have big hair. (The '80s are over!)

A man over 30 should never...

25. Give names to his private body parts.

26. A man over 30 should never:

wear pants low enough to reveal the brand of his underwear.

27. A man over 30 should never:

wear baseball caps backwards.

28. A man over 30 should never:

Share alcohol with pets.

29. A man over 30 should never:

wear more than one article of clothing with a sports team logo on it.

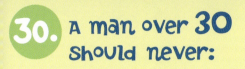

30. A man over 30 should never:

Hang black light posters on his walls.

31. A man over 30 should never:

Rely on someone else to feed, clothe, or bandage him.

32. A man over 30 should never:

wear ponytails. (This goes double if he's gray or follicularly challenged.)

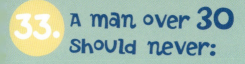

33. A man over 30 should never:

watch cartoons without any children present.

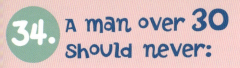
34. A man over **30** should never:

Live with his parents for any reason other than house arrest.

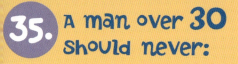

Require house arrest.

36. A man over 30 should never:

Skateboard.

37. A man over **30** should never:

Name pets after LORD OF THE RINGS characters.

38. A man over 30 should never:

Know all the characters in the Marvel universe.

39. A man over 30 should never:

Read the comics first.

40. A man over **30** should never:

Suck the filling out of a snack cake.

41. A man over 30 should never:

Leave .2 ml of milk in a carton and put it back in the fridge.

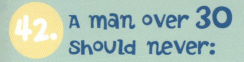

42. A man over 30 should never:

Play air guitar.

43. A man over **30** should never:

Suck helium from balloons.